HOLLOWAY

HOLLOWAY

Robert Macfarlane,
Stanley Donwood
& Dan Richards

faber and faber

First published by Quive-Smith Editions in 2012
This edition first published by Faber and Faber Ltd in 2013
Bloomsbury House
74–77 Great Russell Street
London WC1B 3DA

Typeset by Faber and Faber Ltd
Printed and bound by TJ International Ltd, Padstow, Cornwall

A CIP record for this book
is available from the British Library

ISBN 978-0-571-30271-0

FSC
www.fsc.org
MIX
Paper from
responsible sources
FSC® C013056

4 6 8 10 9 7 5

In memory of
ROGER DEAKIN
1943–2006

Hol weg.

Holwy.

Holway.

Holeway.

Holewaye.

Hollowy.

Holloway.

Holloway – the hollow way. A sunken path, a deep & shady lane. A route that centuries of foot-fall, hoof-hit, wheel-roll & rain-run have harrowed into the land. A track worn down *by the traffic of ages & the fretting of water*, and in places *reduced sixteen or eighteen feet beneath the level of the fields*.

Holloways do not exist on the unyielding rock regions of the archipelago, where the paths stay high, riding the hard surface of the land. But where the stone is soft – malmstone, greensand, sandstone, chalk – there are many to be found, some of them more ravines than roads.

They are landmarks that speak of habit rather than of suddenness. Like creases in the hand, or the wear on the stone sill of a doorstep or stair, they are the result of repeated human actions. Their age chastens without crushing. They relate to other old paths & tracks in the landscape – ways that still connect place to place & person to person.

Greenways, droveways, stanways, stoweys, bradways, whiteways, reddaways, radways, rudways, halsways, roundways, trods, foot-paths, field-paths, leys, dykes, drongs, sarns, snickets, bostles, shutes, driftways, lichways, sandways, ridings, halter-paths, cart-ways, carneys, causeways, here-paths – & also fearways, danger-ways, coffin-paths, corpseways & ghostways.

Many of those who have walked these old ways have seen them as places within which one might *slip back out of this world,* or within which ghosts softly flock. Edward Thomas spoke of hearing the voices of long-dead Roman soldiers as he walked an ancient trackway near Trawsfynydd in Wales. In Hampshire, where a stand of aspens whispered at the cross-roads of two old paths, he listened to the speech of a vanished village: *the ringing of hammer, shoe, & anvil* from the smithy, *the clink, the hum, the roar, the random singing* from the inn.

In 1689 the Japanese poet Basho followed his narrow path to the far north, & as he walked he spoke often with the long-dead poets of the past, including his twelfth-century forebear Saigyo, such that he came afterwards to describe his travels as conversations between *a ghost and a ghost-to-be.*

In 1937 the artist Eric Ravilious visited Gilbert White's parish of Selborne in Hampshire & walked the deep holloways that seam that landscape. He made an engraving of the entrance to one of the holloways – engraving itself a kind of track-making, an incision down into the box-wood or the copper – which shows the entrance to a deep lane, over which the trees are leaning & locking. This entrance to the underworld is guarded by a barn owl, white as the paper upon which it is printed. The owl's head is turned out towards the viewer – its eyes sentinel behind its knight's visor of feathers.

One need not be a mystic to accept that certain old paths are linear only in a simple sense. Like trees, they have branches & like rivers they have tributaries. They are rifts within which time might exist as pure surface, prone to recapitulation & rhyme, weird morphologies, uncanny doublings.

Walking such paths, you might walk up strange pasts. This in the hunter's sense of 'walking up' – meaning *to flush out, to disturb what is concealed.*

The oldest holloways date back to the Iron Age. None is younger than 300 years old. Most holloways begin as ways to markets, to the sea, or to sites of pilgrimage, *lanes worn down by the pack-horses of a hundred generations*. Some were boundary markers, & their routes therefore survive as word-maps in Anglo-Saxon charters:

> From the ford along the herepath to Wulfric's corner; & from the corner along the fence to the unknown water-course, then to the bare stump; & from the bare stump along the fence to the great maple-tree, & then to the hedgerow apple-tree, & then to the herepath, & at last south to the holloway. Along the ditch south to the hollow watercourse, along the watercourse & up to the herepath, & along the herepath to the wheel ford once again.

Few holloways are in use now: they are too narrow and slow to suit modern travel, too deep to be filled in & farmed over. They exist – but cryptically. They have thrown up their own defences and disguises: nettles & briars guard their entrances, trees to either side bend over them & lace their topmost branches to form a tunnel or roof. On their sides, between the tree roots that snake *grotesque & wild*, grow the umbrals: hart's tongue fern, shining cranesbill, ivy & *moschatel, the lover of shade*.

This book is about a holloway & its shades, & a clear map of the holloway's finding is not contained within it.

In July 2004, I travelled with my friend Roger Deakin – swimmer; writer; naturalist; collector; worker with wood; writer of books; maker of friends – to explore the holloways of south Dorset.

These were among the things we carried with us: the novel *Rogue Male,* published by Geoffrey Household in 1939; a map of the area; two tents; a trenching tool; penknives (Roger's blunt, mine blunter); matches & candles; two hipflasks (one of whisky, one of arak).

The holloway we set out to find sits in the horseshoe of the Chideock Valley, cupped by *a half-moon of low green rabbit-cropped hills, the horns of which rest upon the sea.* The Chideock Valley sits within the Marshwood Vale. The Marshwood Vale sits within a further hoop of hills, rising to the high ground of Pilsdon Pen – a chalk summit of 277 metres, ringed by an Iron Age hill-fort.

Imagined from the north, therefore, from Pilsdon Pen, the Chideock holloway exists as a hollow set within a hollow set within a hollow – all of these hollows sloping south towards the sea & the shade of each in turn deepening the shade of the other.

Rogue Male was our guide to the holloway's location. Household's novel is about a man who – fleeing the mysterious pursuers intent on killing him – decides to go to ground in Dorset, somewhere in the half-moon of hills that encircle Chideock. He searches out a deep holloway that he had discovered earlier in his life, its bottom *a cart's width across &* its sides, *with the banks, the hedges above them, & young oaks leaping up front the hedge . . . were fifty feet of blackness.*

Anyone who wishes can dive under the sentinel thorns at the entrance, Household had written, *and push his way through . . . But who would wish?* It is, he warned, *a lane not marked on the map.*

Roger & I set out from the village of North Chideock to find Household's holloway. The blue July air hot & dry. Dust puffing from the road at our footfall; the smell of charred stone. Gold-blaze & rubber-shine from the yellow laurels that bordered the roads of North Chideock.

Only a few hundred yards from the car, where the tarmac began to run to its end, we found a small Catholic chapel of pale stone in the Romanesque style, set back amid oak trees. Roger pushed open its huge front door of ridged & bolt-studded oak. The door opened with an ease that belied its weight, its bottom edge gliding above the flagstones of the porch that were dipped and worn by the passage of many feet.

The air inside the church was cool, & the sandstone of its walls chill to the touch. There was a faint odour of must & everywhere the glint of gilt. Sun-pillars fell at a slant from high windows. *To Illuminate The Church, please place in meter slot £1 coin for 30 mins approx of light.*

The Chideock Valley has a recusant past. After the act of Supremacy in 1558 banned Catholic priests from Britain, missionaries began to re-infiltrate England to keep the faith alive. Several returned to the Chideock Valley & a high-stakes game of hide-&-seek began: the priests fugitive in the landscape, hiding in the woods & holloways; soldiers hunting for them & their supplicants.

The recusancy persisted for around fifty years. In the course of that half-century, five laymen & two priests were caught, tortured & executed. Among them was William Pike, *a simple country man & Chideock carpenter,* who was converted by Father Thomas Pilchard *& became his inseparable companion.* Arrested, tried as a convert & condemned as a traitor, during his execution Pike *was so strong that after he was cut down from the gibbet he stood up again & had to be thrust down & held by soldiers so that the butchery could continue.*

Hugh Green was arrested at Lyme Regis as he attempted to go to France, taken to Dorchester, tried & condemned. On 4 July 1642 he suffered *considerable barbarity, but remained conscious throughout the process of being hanged, drawn & quartered.* Eventually he was beheaded & *his head used as a football by the incensed mob.*

Father Cornelius ascended the scaffold at Dorchester, kissed the gallows, uttered the words of St Andrew – *O Cross, long desired – & prayed for his executioner & the queen* as the rope was placed around his neck.

Immediately after the execution of Father Pilchard, *Dorchester was beset with violent storms, which many took to be a judgement.*

We left the chapel & followed the road to its end & then picked up an old path leading into the hills, which was clearly the beginning of the holloway, for it was soon cut down ten feet or more into the caramel sandstone. Heavy rain had fallen the previous week & the holloway floor bore evidence of water-rush. Here & there patches of smooth surface stone had been rinsed clean & exposed, so that they lay glowing in their first sunlight for 200 million years.

Moving up into the hills, we checked & re-checked the descriptions in *Rogue Male,* but the landscape of the novel would not quite fit the landscape itself. There was a mismatch, slight but unmistakable. The directions of finding had been encrypted by Household.

Near the summit of the half-moon of hills, the path became so overgrown with nettles and brambles that we were unable to progress. We scrambled up its steep eastern side & into *the pollinous air of the flower meadow that bordered it,* from where the holloway we had been following was almost invisible. Then, by the side of a high old ash tree, we found a way back down into the holloway & so there we passed through that hole in the hedge & descended into the holloway's depth, using ivy as a rope to abseil down the sandstone sides & into the shade.

The bright hot surface world was forgotten. So close was the latticework of leaves & branches & so high the eastern side of the holloway that light penetrated its depths only in thin lances. We came occasionally to small clearings, where light fell & grass grew. In the windless warm air, groups of flies bobbed & weaved, each dancing around a set point like vibrating atoms held in a matrix.

At one point we could see far along the holloway to the north, the curves of the walls holding the lens of empty light at its end. The view down a rifled barrel; an eye to the keyhole; a glimpse into the shade-world.

You could live undisturbed and undetected here for a long time, said Roger.

Later, after our first exploration of the main holloway, we set out on a wider reconnaissance of the area. We camouflaged our rucksacks with bracken & branch, climbed out of the holloway at the old ash tree & emerged into the meadow. The grass blades flashed like steel in the sun & we stood blinking & wringing the light from our eyes.

That afternoon we walked the curved ridge of hills that makes up the rest of the half-moon: Copper Hill, Denhay Hill, Jan's Hill. Everywhere we saw evidence of creatures taking refuge in the soil: mason bees, wasps, rabbits, successors to the fugitive priests & the hunted man. There were networks of burrows through the gorsy undergrowth: miniature green holloways, no bigger in cross-section than a croquet hoop, made by badgers.

Hours after, as the air was hazing up, we returned to our holloway hide-out, dropping down by the old ash-tree into the near-darkness. We cleared nettles and briars, moved loose trunks to make seats. We cut holly staffs with our penknives; the fresh wood hard and pale to the blade. Roger built an almost smokeless fire with a hot centre of tinder, on which we cooked. Firelight flickered off the holloway walls & set complicated shadows moving in the leaves & the day seemed to convene itself about the furnace-point of the flames. We told stories, read out passages from *Rogue Male. I remind myself that I have extended and presumably will extend again in the time of the outer world.*

Down in the dusk of the holloway, the landscape's pasts felt excitingly alive & coexistent, as if history had pleated back on itself, bringing discontinuous moments into contact & creating correspondences that survived as a territorial imperative to concealment, escape & encounter.

After full nightfall, Roger & I pitched our tents on the flower meadow, behind a hedge & below the slope of Copper Hill & lay on our backs, looking up at the sky as the stars came fast & then faster. *A shooting star, there! Another, & then another.*

The next morning, a little after dawn, I climbed to the top of Copper Hill. There was an ocean of mist, filling the half-moon of hills & beyond the ocean of mist lay the sea itself to the south. The mist bred mirages of figures moving within it & the heat bred mirages over & upon the water, offering false promises of islands & mountain ranges.

Roger & I walked south and downhill, out of the holloway, off the half-moon of hills, down into the mist, past the chapel hidden in the laurels & down to the coast, where a pebble beach shelves steeply away from high sandstone cliffs.

The sea was warm so we swam, backstroking out for a hundred yards or so & then treading water. We looked back at the ochre sandstone cliffs & the green hills rising behind them & our arms and legs moving like phantom limbs beneath the surface of the blue, blue sea.

In August 2006, Roger died. He died many years too young. The day of his death I went with two friends to the pine-forests of Holkham in North Norfolk. The light in the deepest stands of the pines was like dusk, and the air smelt resinous, spicy. We slept among the trees & at dawn and dusk we walked across the gold & open beach to swim in big, steady waves. For miles along the wrack-line lay razor-shells in their millions.

In September 2011, I returned to the Dorset holloway with two friends, Dan Richards & Stanley Donwood.

These were among the things we carried: a copy of Geoffrey Household's *Rogue Male*. The map that Roger & I had taken to the holloway. Two rucksacks & a pair of saddle-bags, a hip-flask, two penknives, matches & candles. A bottle of damson gin.

We parked at Pilsdon Pen & walked through Lob Gate, steeply up towards the summit of the Pen. White chalk, sharp flint, the purple of ling, the green of gorse & yellow stars of tormentil. Halfway up its slopes we passed into a thick & enfolding mist which we had not seen from its base & within that mist we each swiftly became a ghost to the other.

There were times, as I walked the ramparts of the hill fort widdershins, Stan walked them deasilwise & Dan stepped across their centre, when each of us moved lost in our own luminous socket of mist & there were times when we showed as silhouettes & times when our paths crossed & we emerged into focus, before shifting away again.

Once, I dropped down into the wide path that ran between the ramparts, the path that was sunk down within them & to which they provided the walls & I experienced the powerful illusion that the path was sloping away and downhill ahead of me & not running to an end or continuing its own progress, but rather fraying down & out into the mist & offering an invitation to descend.

From Pilsdon Pen it was down, steeply down, into the Marshwood Vale & from the Marshwood Vale it was up, steeply up, on high-sided lanes, until at last we found a path across the ridge of the west side of *the half-moon of hills* & that path felt like a borehole through the ridge rather than a passage over it, for it was so overgrown that it was more tunnel than path. We emerged out of its darkness into the Chideock Valley & almost immediately Dan fell off his bike & then stood up laughing from the verge.

That long & happy day passed in exploration, tree-climbing, walking, talking, lounging. I had not gone in search of Roger's shade, but I found him there nonetheless, glimpsed startlingly clearly at the turn of a corner or the edge of a tree-line. Actual memory traces existed in the stumps of the holly saplings we had cut as staffs, our blade-marks still visible in the wood. *He knowth hym by the traces & by his denne and by the soole.*

I now understand it certainly to be the case, though I have long imagined it to be true, that stretches of a path might carry memories of a person just as a person might of a path.

In the flower meadow below Copper Hill, near an old flat oak, I read out poems by Edward Thomas, who was the great twentieth-century poet of the old way, as Paul Nash was its great twentieth-century artist. Thomas walked thousands of miles along paths, from the famous (Sarn Helen in Wales, the Icknield Way & the Ridgeway in the chalk counties of southern England) to the local (Old Litton Lane & Harepath Lane, near his Hampshire home). His poems are thronged with ghosts, doubles & paths that peter out. He understood himself in topographical terms & he saw that paths run through people as surely as they run through places.

Many a road and track
That, since the dawn's first crack,
Up to the forest brink,
Deceived the travellers
Suddenly now blurs
And in they sink.

– o –

Late that night, we cycled back up to the holloway in fierce silver rain, skidding on wet mud, raindrops showing in our headlamp beams & the eye-glow of unknown animals glinting in the hedgerows.

The eyes of creatures shine in low light because of the presence of the *tapetum lucidum,* the bright carpet, a mirror-like membrane of iridescent cells that sits behind the retina. Light passes first through the rod & cone cells then strikes the membrane & rebounds back through the retina towards the light source. Any available light is used twice to see with; perception is thereby doubled.

So heavy was the rain and so thick the blackness of the night, that we soon became separated, each invisible to the other & yet when we later spoke, each of us had had the experience of being pursued by another who was not of our group – someone holding a bright light & following in our tracks.

We slept that night down in the depths of the holloway. In the darkest hours of the night a rain storm came, the water falling so hard it left drill-holes in the leaf-litter. Waking at dawn I found that I had left my copy of Edward Thomas's poems unsheltered. The rain had plumped it & driven gobbets of earth & shards of leaf in between its pages:

> *The path, winding like silver, trickles on,*
> *Bordered and even invaded by thinnest moss*
> *. . . and the eye*
> *Has but the road, the wood that overhangs*
> *And underyawns it, and the path that looks*
> *As if it led on to some legendary*
> *Or fancied place where men have wished to go*
> *And stay; till, sudden, it ends where the wood ends.*

After full sunrise we walked and bicycled down to the coast at Seatown & there we climbed Ridge Cliff and Doghouse Hill in a high & golden light & a strong white wind. We climbed them barefoot, fitting our feet into the print-trails that had been dipped into the turf by earlier walkers, & the earth was warm and finely graded within each print. To our west was the Undercliff, & Lyme Regis round the bay. White-sailed yachts scooted eastwards on the big wind; Stan's hat was snatched from his head by the wind.

Later that day, before we left the valley, we went to the Catholic chapel in North Chideock. In the visitors' book had been written many prayers & supplications.

29/08/2010 *Please bless Lisa Bevely who was murdered leaving her little boy of five years. Thank you.*

17-July-2011 *Pray for my two friends who are ill, Joshua Davies and Sue Holloway.*

25th August '10 *Please bless a good friend who has not long left us, may he rest in peace.*

Pilsdon Pen

Looking out from the lower turf ramparts of Pilsdon Pen we sight a crescent moon of hills – a vein within a leaf spring – arcing to the coast. Somewhere in there lies our quarry; a lane diving into the dark.

An inky eye, an ammonite.
A hollow, foot-querned way.

Turning away from the sea we begin to scale the hill. Over the stile, spiralling up between tussocks and gorse, stepping through the sudden cloud-line into thickly mantled murk. A lichen souper. Up until we clamber out on a floating island steppe – a layered mist rolling about our three glades in the fog. There is a trig: there, silent cattle; here, earthworks – mounds and humps.

All elsewhere is milk.
A void.

We spread out to search our margins: Rob to the left, Stan to the right, me down the middle of the dim flat top. We do not orchestrate this trident sweep but each, finding himself alone, determines to carry on through the ether, round the worked ellipse, skirting the moat, to the point we'll surely converge . . . on the edge of the fern-table brume.

A fume quoit caught on this whittled marl peg.

Walking out purblind, vision penned and closing down – sapped, as a migraine pinches the light – I can hear nothing but the damp air pool and pass, tendril fog-weed fringing-in to clag my ears in unnatural silence. I stump on.

Then I begin to see things. I hear the doldrum sirens call – fine and far away.

There.

Beguiling; warm; inviting; sad.

Strange; familiar.

'Where are my friends?' I ponder, vaguely. 'How long have I been...'

Then I fall off the world.

Back down in the particular we unstrap our bikes.

The car. That strap. My bike. This. The tactile reassurance of the close at hand. Sunlight falls and kestrels call to disavow what we'd just seen and been through and, indeed, the clouds seem to have lifted off and melted quite away when we turn and look back.

Stan and I plunge down the brink and speed. The rifled lanes spill past and we grin tight until, turn approaching, brakes applied – and now, and now; no, come on; now – I begin a slow crash into Dorset with its gleaming chalk and plough-turned flint-tipped ruts.

Holloway

Sat above the dry den shute in a silver flat-grained dusk, I listen to the others talking – out of sight, away down in the dip. Yesterday, we hid our belongings in the pleats of the old road's bed – the bicycles and bivvy bags half-buried in the drifts of blanket mulch.

My bicycle did not take well to the rough farm tracks and bridleways. Tyres too thin, gears too high – a frail old racehorse forced to plough – soon the chain was broken and the gears bent out of shape . . . Maybe I should have abandoned it here, I thought; lost on a long-forgotten road – black frame left to flake and moulder under trunks grown pinguid-fat round broken old barbed wire.

It is late September and the day is mostly ebbed.

This morning we ate tea-bread and drank violet damson gin from the bottle. We stretched and yawned, the sleep still in our eyes, flat earth smell on our hands. Waking in the holloway the thing that struck me, lying half out of my green cocoon and staring up – staring through the awning mesh of twigs and stems – was the way their patterns shone white when I blinked or turned away. A fretted photo-negative weaving with the vessels in my eye.

Burnt in. Of a piece.

Once up, we sat round in the bank, ears pricked. We slept well but for the rain at four, faintly aware of the bird song swell with the sun – the hedges here are stuffed with birds; abundant, loud and brazen-bright as we are out of place. We hide ourselves as émigrés, as artificers in a trench, sat with our sub rosa gin below the parapet.

Some 250 miles east, in an archive box, I found a card:

As an only child, the sheer solitude of the hero's escape and odyssey appealed to me. He was a swimmer too, dragged his tortured body into the Rhine like an otter – throwing off the guard-dogs that pursued him.

Down in the next valley's pub, we sit beside the cheerful fire and talk: nursing pints, mindful of the cold outside and the dark walk home to our deep burrow sacks.

On the way back, I recall the lady stood on the hill behind our hide whose blank stare caught and pinned us as we climbed into the world this morning, whilst her dog – quite forgotten – ran circles. Her red jacket, madder red – her frown of vexed mistrust.

Later, three lights dazzle up and we all start and scramble into the ditch, for fear of lamping, hardwired fright of the hunted, the trees shot through and blazing – men come to pick us off.

Yet, when we woke again next day – everything as it should be; three men in a hedge – we agreed the episode seemed spectral and unreal. A shared night terror dreamt up in the wake of old ale dregs . . . but what of these scuffed marks, here; these hurried flails cut in the fosse? These thrashing breaks for cover in the boundary of the bank?

Martyrs

The bees that tunnel in the rock and hard-packed mud of the walls here go back a long way.

Holed-up underneath the thread-work of the vaulting ash, thin holly, beech and suckered elms – sinew peeling, shot through with poison galleries – I peer into the bee maze, stood down among the rib roots and moss.

The bees still mass in the *hola weg* and drone down in the valley church, the gilded Queen of martyrs, beside the aged books and pitch mantraps.

Records of steel barbs in the hollow, hooded troops cast out to snare a covert congregation – creeping round the black-wood crescent; lamping with dark lanterns. No moon above the whispering fields, low service in the cross-hatched apse and every outside sound an ambush. Amphidromic points of faith.

The holloway is absence; a wood-way worn away by buried feet. Regressing back into the mind, an ink-preoccupation set amongst the forests of Northern Europe and the bright beast tapestry of the hunt. Walking, hiding, running man, huddled in the lee of a tree – a tree amongst trees, a way among ways – brief safety in the sunken lull. Flayed into tingling life by the hopeless desire to love.

In the burnished little church, four hollow men gaze out to us from flaking plaster frescos. Becher silo faces.

Stark, composed – but one's eyes focus off, preoccupied – as if by bees.

Hol weg.

Holwy.

Holway.

Holeway.

Holewaye.

Hollowy.

Holloway.

The first edition of this book was printed using newly-cast type by Richard Lawrence at his Oxford workshop.

277 copies were printed, as that is the height in metres above sea-level of Pilsdon Pen, the iron age hill-fort where the book was begun.

QUIVE-SMITH